CW00401200

100 Rants on Why Men are Pants

Amy Charter

summersdale

100 RANTS ON WHY MEN ARE PANTS
1st edition printed in 2000
This 2nd edition published by Summersdale Publishers Ltd © 2004

Summersdale Publishers Ltd
46 West Street
Chichester
West Sussex
PO19 1RP
United Kingdom

www.summersdale.com

ISBN 1 84024 420 8

Printed and bound in Belgium

Cartoons by Kate Taylor

Pants by Rob Smith

'The male is a domestic animal which, if treated with firmness, can be trained to do most things.'

Jilly Cooper

Introduction

Why men are pants: a large tome would barely scratch the surface of such an extensive topic. But, for your convenience, here is a handy and concise pocket book with just the right amount of ammunition to fire at the nearest male – and get him where it hurts.

Whether you are a woman and want to pin-point exactly what it is that gets your goat about men, or whether you are a man who would like to learn how to improve himself (unlikely), you will enjoy these tongue-in-cheek nuggets of wisdom. Oh, and a last word to any man reading this – don't go into a sulk, will you?

- Menstruation
- Mental Illness
- Menopause
- Meningitis

Discomfort and illness
always start with men.

Women like cats.

Men say they like cats, but when
women aren't looking, men kick cats.

Men have selective hearing. There are certain keywords (football, sex, food, beer etc.) that he will hear, but on the whole it is futile trying to get a man to absorb anything you say.

Toilets, anniversaries, and erogenous zones all have one thing in common. Men always miss them.

BEWARE: When you enter into a relationship with a man, not far behind him will be his possessive, son-worshipping, death-defying mother.

Single women complain that all the good
men are married, while married women
complain about their lousy husbands.
This confirms that there is no
such thing as a good man.

Men in drag: who on earth can understand why anyone, given a comfortable alternative, would *choose* to don a skimpy dress, red lipstick and excruciatingly high heels?

Never ask a man to report back on what a bride was wearing at a wedding; the only answer you will get is, 'A dress.'

Grooms always look the same.
It is the bride who attracts
all the attention.

Whilst it is pitiful that men have a strong desire to compare genital size with one another, it must be emphasised that size *does* matter. Small penises are crap.

A man's life expectancy is 20 per cent shorter than a woman's – it's that same old story: he just can't last the distance.

Watching a man dance is like watching a
rabid dog trying to escape
from a small cage.

19

Men are sensitive creatures. You will find in particular two areas of concern: his ego and his genitalia. Both are susceptible to pain.

Men are five times more
likely to kill themselves
than women. Pathetic.

God made Adam as a practice model.
He perfected the human form
when he made Eve.

Men's definition of safe sex
is a padded headboard.

Gentlemen – give the love-bites a miss.
A woman does not really want her neck
to look as though it has been savaged
by next door's Doberman.

Black Widow spiders have the right idea. They kill their men after mating and so stop the snoring before it starts.

The male performance: the reason Viagra
was invented. And while on the subject
of a poor act, premature ejaculation:
just when you thought it was
getting good – it's all over.

A man reaches his sexual peak in life
before he knows what to do with it.

Women have more erogenous zones
than men and yet men can't seem
to locate a single one.

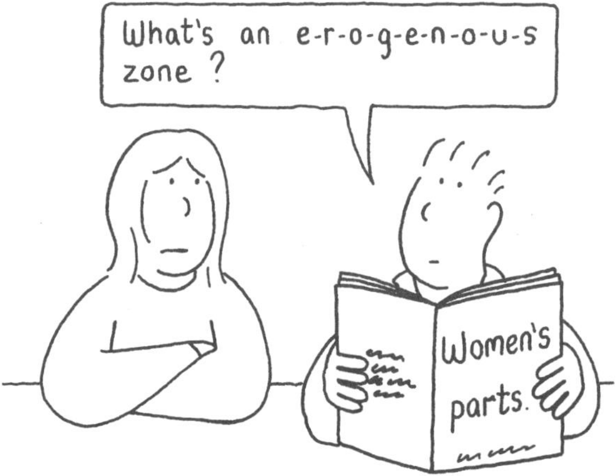
What's an e-r-o-g-e-n-o-u-s zone ?
Women's parts.

A man's definition of foreplay is taking your knickers off.

Why doesn't a man understand that kissing him on a Sunday morning is like kissing a pan scourer soaked in beer?

A man is a discerning creature. He will only choose to have sex with a woman if she breathes.

Why is it that, just when you think you
have met Mr Right, he takes
his trousers down to reveal
a pair of truly offensive
Y-fronts? Game Over.

Electric lawn mowers were
invented so that men could
find their way back to the house.

Even if a man has everything,
he will always need a woman
to show him how to work it.

A man only ever says anything intelligent
when he uses as a precursor,
'My wife/girlfriend says...'

BEWARE: Men are too chicken to make a clean break from a relationship. A man will simply behave so badly that a woman will finish it first. Said man will disappear, leaving in his wake a woman furnished with an all-consuming guilt.

Men are liable to starve
without a tin-opener.

Only a man would economise on buying
a car just so he could install that essential
piece of motoring equipment,
the stereo, worth at least
three times its host's value.

Men are afraid of cosmetic instruments.
For extra peace of mind, always
keep a pair of eyelash curlers
under your pillow.

The length, potency and audibility of a
man's fart are to him and his male friends
the measure of his worth.
Need we say more?

A man will wait until the fridge is empty except for half a tin of baked beans and a beer. For two weeks he will survive on take-aways and then think about refilling it – with beer.

Men do not appear to possess sufficient
intelligence to enable them to replace
the toilet seat in its rightful,
horizontal position.

Diamonds are a woman's best friend,
dogs are a man's best friend. I think we
can gather which of the sexes
is more intelligent.

Men are only capable of active thought
for about five minutes of every hour.
Ask him what he is thinking and you'll
have to wait for an answer.

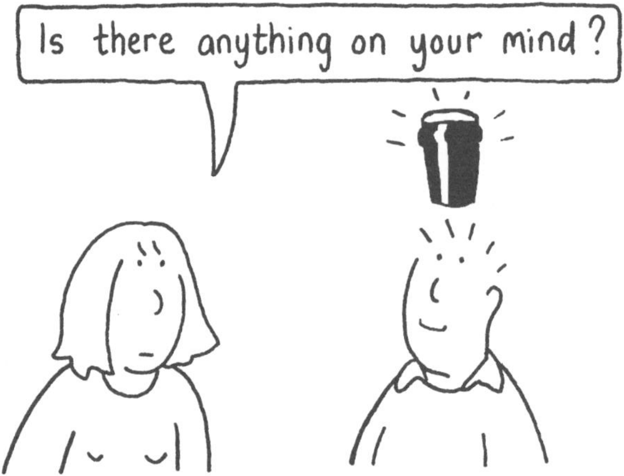
Is there anything on your mind?

Men believe they are capable of
telekinetic powers: if they shout
loudly at the players they WILL
hear and they WILL
take that shot.

Men do not realise the real value of the phone – they see it purely as a means to convey limited, monosyllabic information, therefore failing to discover the potential enjoyment and fulfilment that this instrument can bring.

Men have a pathological obsession with keeping the remote control in their possession. This is because:

a) it is a gadget
b) without it, a man loses that little bit of control that took him so long to cultivate
c) by nature, he is a selfish creature.

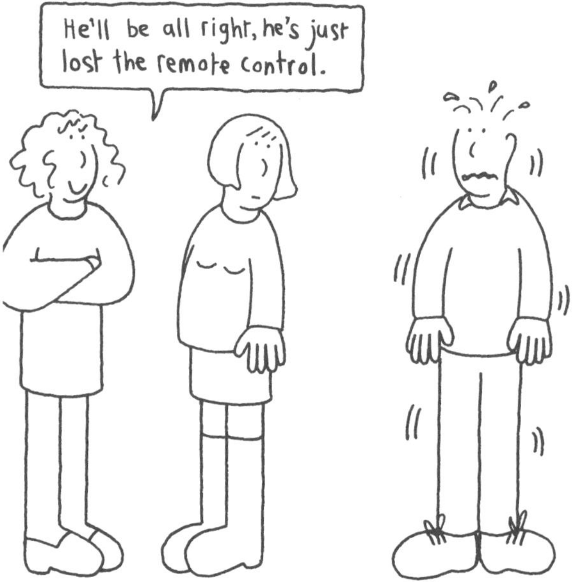
He'll be all right, he's just lost the remote control.

You do not have to go far to find a man a
film he will enjoy. It must simply contain
one, or all, of the following components:
convent girls, nurses, car chases,
gadgets or lesbians — all of which
will drive him to a state
of frenzied excitement.

Men will not go near the kitchen for ten months of the year, but as soon as the barbecue season comes around, he will monopolise the cooking. 'Barbies' are the ideal opportunity for grand machismo: torching the meat and asserting himself over naked flames.

A man's handwriting always reflects his
personality. It is formulated by
the time he is thirteen, and
does not change for
the rest of his life.

Due to psychological inferiority complexes, men actually name their penises. They will call their little friend (the one who does all the thinking) something like 'Rambo' rather than the possibly more appropriate 'Winky'.

Men will not, by default, ask for
directions. This could explain
why Moses was wandering
through the wilderness
for forty years.

Some men become
construction workers so they can
draw attention to themselves from
passing women. To ensure
a positive response a few even
let their trousers expose
most of their buttocks.

Rather than as a delicious food, curries are regarded by men as a passport to an ensuing 'ring-stinger' — something a man must experience in order to exert his true masculinity.

It is rare to find a man who is remotely sensitive. The only men who are sensitive, caring and compassionate have boyfriends.

If you want to dump your man, tell him you love him. If this doesn't work, ask him to marry you. If this doesn't work, tell him you want to have his babies. Now blink, and you will not see him for dust.

Girls grow out of toys by the time they reach their teens – men carry on needing 'gadgets' to play with for the rest of their lives. If it is shiny, has buttons and follows commands, it not only provides endless entertainment but also gives a man status with his friends.

James Bond was created to give men a false sense of identity and something to aspire to. It is normal for a man to think he is Bond when in the car or playing with a gadget such as a personal organiser or the remote control.

Women gain confidence through achievement. Men rarely experience achievement, so gain theirs through a deluded association with their superheroes, often believing they *are* Superman.

The words 'commitment' and 'monogamy' are as repugnant to a man as having his head flushed down a toilet. If, by a strange turn of events, you wish to attract a man and be with him for any amount of time, avoid using these words.

They will never admit it, but men sulk like babies. The male sulk involves extended periods of pouting and silence, as well as the slamming shut, or down, of anything they can get their hands on. It is dangerous to say anything to a man in a sulk.

Women can pay each other compliments; if a man pays another man a compliment his heterosexual friends will know that he is gay.

Men take longer to mature. In fact, most men don't seem to get past adolescence. It is appropriate, therefore, to talk to them as you would a naughty child.

Men's magazines often feature pictures of naked women. Women's magazines also feature pictures of naked women. This is because the female body is beautiful and sleek, whereas the male body is lumpy and hairy.

72

It's Saturday morning and you run a hot bubble bath. The bathroom seemed perfectly normal when you left it; now there is a malodorous smell permeating the atmosphere. The culprit can be found lying in bed and smiling smugly, as he reads the sports section of his favourite paper.

Never be lulled into thinking that a man is above the attractions of a soft porn magazine. He may act nonchalant when you are around, but when with friends he will pore over the magazine, salivating with excitement.

74

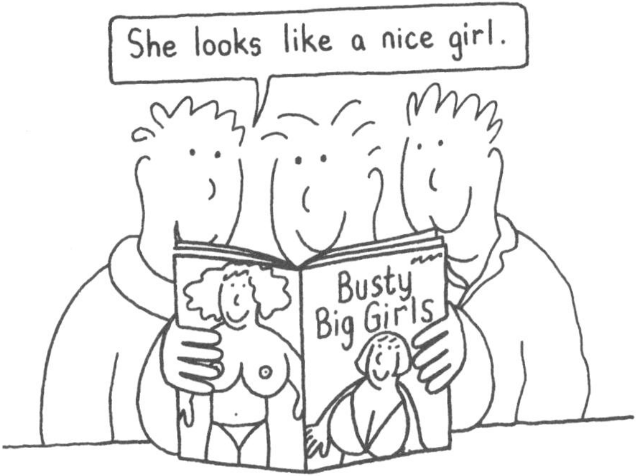
She looks like a nice girl.
Busty Big Girls

Although acceptable habits in small children and dogs, a man shovelling food into his mouth at a rate of knots, chewing with slack jaw and dribbling, is not someone you want to be seen in a restaurant with.

Women realise that urinating, for a man, is very clever. But how difficult can it be to direct the urine into the toilet?

The male of the species displays a tendency to stare vacantly into the middle distance while readjusting/ scratching his scrotal region – a charming habit, which it is a pleasure to be exposed to.

Men only realise their pants and socks
need to be washed when a
strange fungal substance forms
on the insides.

Men are unable to enjoy the art form
that is gossiping. He will only be
interested if you are telling him
about your two female best friends
making love to each other.

Whilst a woman's Saturday night in may involve a good book, good food and a deep bath, a man's would include a football game or, more typically, extensive lists of football results.

Men have a fanatical desire to arrange their possessions in alphabetical order; and the saddest cases have also been known to catalogue said possessions. Take particular heed when you see a man using his personal organiser to do this.

Golf. Men who don't play this game differ little from those who do. They are still obsessed with the length of their club, the distance of their shot, and whether they can get a hole in one.

Men buy a newspaper purely to get excited/depressed about the latest sports result/property prices/car prices – and you are treated to a loud running commentary. Your response must be highly animated, or you may be exposed to one of his sulks.

A man will plead grave illness and go
to bed at the first sign of a headache.
However, he is never too ill to
fantasize that Nursey-Nursey
will come and look after him.

There is a form of the male species which fails to understand that a woman's breasts will never be great conversationalists.

Men lie 99 per cent of the time. The
only time they tell the truth is
when it is the most
tactless thing to do.

A mild pheromonal smell can be attractive, but five days' stale sweat will attract only bluebottles and post-match rugby players

Men are incapable of childbirth. Even if they were the ones having babies, their fear about the prospect of pain would probably mean the end of the human race.

Men have a misguided view of
what counts as helping
with the housework.

The ultimate reason why men are pants?

Because they're not women!